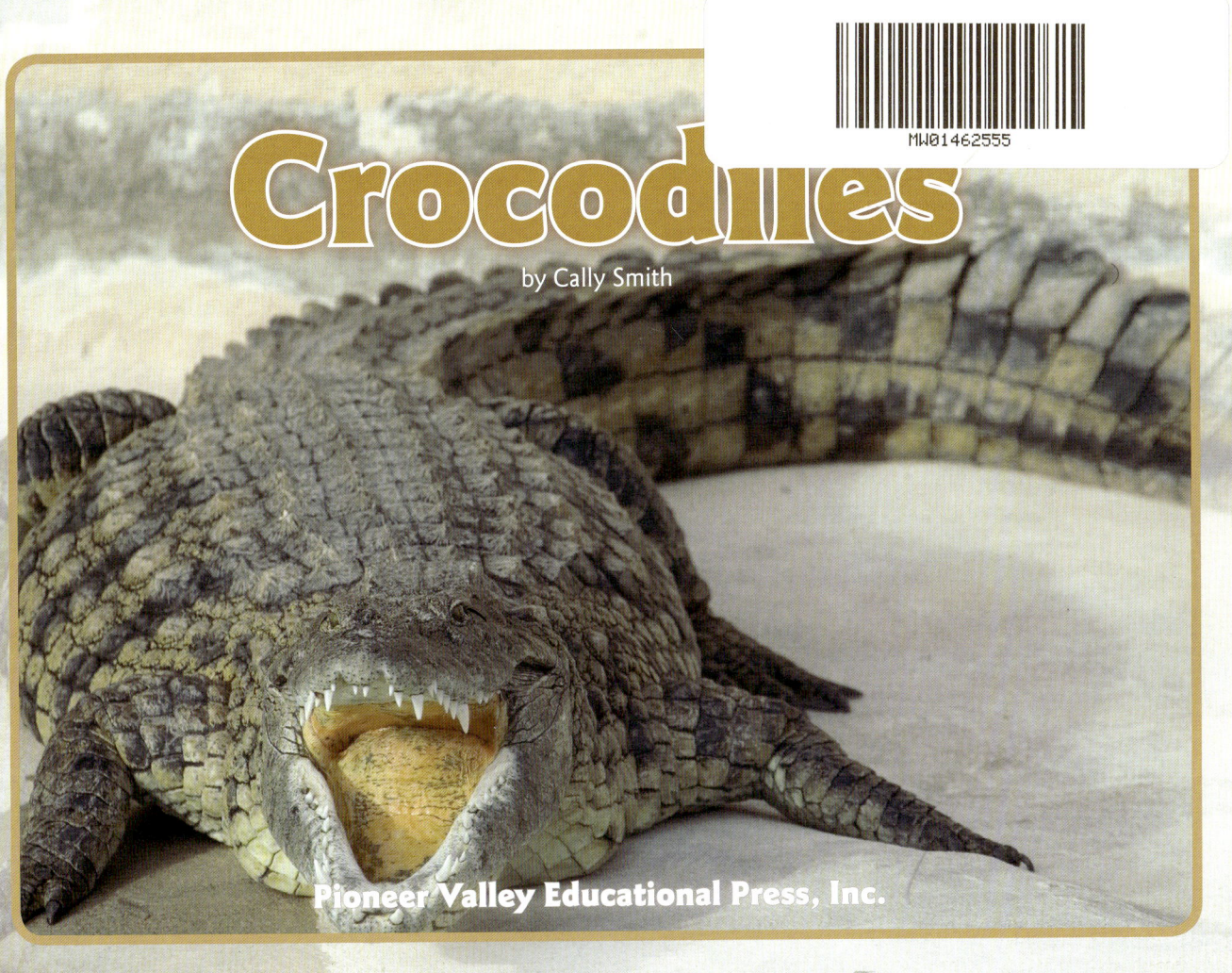

Crocodiles

by Cally Smith

Pioneer Valley Educational Press, Inc.

This is a crocodile.
Crocodiles look like giant lizards.
A crocodile can be as long as 15 feet.

3

Crocodiles have powerful **jaws**. They have the strongest bite of any animal. Their sharp teeth grab and hold onto **prey**.

5

Crocodiles have long bodies and long tails that help them swim fast. They have webbed feet. Crocodiles use their webbed feet to make fast turns in the water. Their webbed feet also help crocodiles to walk in **shallow** water.

Crocodiles can move fast on land. They **slither** on their bellies like a snake. When they slither, they whip their tails from side to side.

Mother crocodiles dig shallow holes and build nests out of mud, sand, and weeds. Crocodiles lay 40 to 60 eggs in their nests.

Baby crocodiles make a loud cry when they are hatching. The mother crocodile comes and digs them out of the nest. She carries them to the water in her mouth. Sometimes baby crocodiles are eaten by raccoons, birds, and crabs. Even adult crocodiles eat baby crocodiles.

jaws: the part of the mouth that holds the teeth

prey: an animal hunted for food

shallow: not deep

slither: to slide along a surface